DO YOU REALLY WANT TO MEET SPINOSAURUS?

BY ANNETTE BAY PIMENTEL • ILLUSTRATED BY DANIELE FABBRI

AMICUS ILLUSTRATED and **AMICUS INK**
are published by Amicus
P.O. Box 1329, Mankato, MN 56002
www.amicuspublishing.us

EDITOR: Alissa Thielges
SERIES DESIGNER: Kathleen Petelinsek
BOOK DESIGNER: Veronica Scott

LIBRARY OF CONGRESS CATALOGING-IN-PUBLICATION DATA
Names: Pimentel, Annette Bay, author. | Fabbri, Daniele, 1978- Illustrator.
Title: Do you really want to meet spinosaurus? / by Annette Bay Pimentel ; illustrated by Daniele Fabbri.
Description: Mankato, Minnesota : Amicus Ink, [2020] | Series: Do you really want to meet a dinosaur? | Audience: K to grade 3.
Identifiers: LCCN 2018031881 (print) | LCCN 2018036662 (ebook) | ISBN 9781681517896 (pdf) | ISBN 9781681517070 (library binding) | ISBN 9781681524931 (pbk.)
Subjects: LCSH: Spinosaurus--Juvenile literature.
Classification: LCC QE862.S3 (ebook) | LCC QE862.S3 P559 2020 (print) | DDC 567.912--dc23
LC record available at https://lccn.loc.gov/2018031881

Printed in the United States of America
HC 10 9 8 7 6 5 4 3 2 1
PB 10 9 8 7 6 5 4 3 2 1

ABOUT THE AUTHOR
Annette Bay Pimentel lives in Moscow, Idaho with her family. She doesn't have a time machine, so she researches the past at the library. She writes about what happened a long time ago in nonfiction picture books like *Mountain Chef* (2016, Charlesbridge). You can visit her online at www.annettebaypimentel.com.

ABOUT THE ILLUSTRATOR
Daniele Fabbri was born in Ravenna, Italy, in 1978. He graduated from Istituto Europeo di Design in Milan, Italy, and started his career as a cartoon animator, storyboarder, and background designer for animated series. He has worked as a freelance illustrator since 2003, collaborating with advertising agencies and international publishers, including many books for Amicus.

Telling fish stories is one of the best parts of going fishing. Have you told one about Spinosaurus? It was a huge fish-eating dinosaur. Wouldn't you really like to meet a Spinosaurus?

The problem is Spinosaurus is extinct. To meet one, you'll need a time machine. Go back 100 million years, to the Cretaceous Period. Travel to northern Africa, where the Sahara Desert is now. Don't forget boots! It was a swamp back then.

You've arrived! It's hot. You've seen turtles and fish back home.

You can see some here, too!

You don't see a dinosaur yet? Don't worry. Spinosaurus is so huge it will be easy to spot.

See above those bushes? Those are spine-like bones on Spinosaurus's back. They make up the dinosaur's sail. It sticks up 7 feet (2.1 m). The sail may scare away other dinosaurs. Or it may help Spinosaurus attract a mate. Move closer for a better look.

Wow! Spinosaurus is big. It's 50 feet (15 m) long. That's as long as three cars. It is heavy, too.

Scientists aren't sure how much it weighs. They estimate between 8 and 23 tons (7 and 21 metric tons).

Spinosaurus is built to hunt in water. Its flat feet are perfect for walking in mud. Its snout looks like a crocodile's, but it is three times as long. At 6 feet (1.8 m) in length, the snout could easily snap you up! Keep a safe distance from this carnivore.

Spinosaurus slides smoothly into the water. Time for dinner!

Spinosaurus doesn't need a fishing pole to catch fish.

It can sense their movement in the water.

Spinosaurus opens its jaw wide. Its teeth are pointy, good for ripping fish apart. Snap! It snatches up a huge fish. The jaw of Spinosaurus is wide enough to catch large prey.

Is it watching you? Its eyes and nose are perched high on its head. Spinosaurus can see above water and breathe while it swims. You'd think that fish would have filled it up. But maybe it's still hungry. Look how the turtle paddles away fast.

A pterosaur swoops close. Splash! Spinosaurus grabs it right out of the air. Yes, Spinosaurus eats fish. But it will also eat anything else it can grab.

This is a very hungry dinosaur. It keeps eyeing you. You had better leave before it decides to try a nibble. Head back to your time with your biggest fish story yet!

WHERE HAVE SPINOSAURUS FOSSILS BEEN FOUND?

GLOSSARY

carnivore—An animal that eats only meat.

Cretaceous Period—The time period from 145.5 million to 65.5 million years ago.

extinct—No longer found living anywhere in the world; known only from fossils.

prey—An animal hunted and killed for food by another animal.

pterosaur—A flying reptile that lived at the time of dinosaurs.

sail—A body part on a Spinosaurus that rose up from its back, similar to a shark's dorsal fin.

snout—The long front part of an animal's head, including the nose, mouth, and jaw.

swamp—An area with wet, spongy ground that is partially covered in water.

ton—A measure of weight equal to 1,000 pounds (454 kg).

AUTHOR'S NOTE

Too bad for us, time machines aren't real. But all of the details about Spinosaurus in this book are based on research by scientists who study fossils. For example, in 2004 scientists announced they had discovered the tooth of a Spinosaurus deep in a pterosaur vertebra. This fossil proves that Spinosaurus preyed on pterosaurs. New dinosaur discoveries are made every year. Look up the books and websites below to learn more.

READ MORE

Gilbert, Sara. *Spinosaurus.* Mankato, Minn.: Creative Education, 2019.

Levine, Sara C. *Fossil by Fossil: Comparing Dinosaur Bones.* Minneapolis: Millbrook, 2018.

Nardo, Don. *Deadliest Dinosaurs.* San Diego, Calif.: ReferencePoint Press, Inc., 2017.

WEBSITES

DINOSAURS: EXTINCT BUT POWERFUL CREATURES—NATIONAL GEOGRAPHIC KIDS
http://kids.nationalgeographic.com/explore/nature/dinosaurs/
Compare sizes of dinosaurs, meet paleontologists, and more.

PBS KIDS: DINOSAUR GAMES
https://pbskids.org/games/dinosaur/
Play games, watch videos, and try online activities to learn more about these fascinating extinct animals.